LOOk Closer

Reptiles

LONDON, NEW YORK, MUNICH,
MELBOURNE, and DELHI

Text by Sue Malyan
Editor Fleur Star
Senior designer Janet Allis
Publishing manager Susan Leonard
Managing art editor Clare Shedden
Jacket design Simon Oon
Picture researcher Sarah Mills
Production Luca Bazzoli
DTP Designer Almudena Díaz

First American Edition, 2005

Published in the United States by
DK Publishing, Inc.
375 Hudson Street
New York, New York 10014

05 06 07 08 09   10 9 8 7 6 5 4 3 2 1

Copyright © 2005 Dorling Kindersley Limited

A Cataloging-in-Publication record for this book
is available from the Library of Congress.

ISBN 0-7566-1434-1

Color reproduction by Colourscan, Singapore
Printed and bound in China by Hung Hing

Discover more at
www.dk.com

Look for us. We will show
you the size of every
animal in this book.

Contents

Spot and snap

Creeping slowly out of its burrow, this spotted salamander is looking to snap up its dinner.

... A salamander likes to live in a shady place to help its skin stay wet. If its skin dried out, it would die.

My long, thin shape helps me to burrow into the ground.

I think I've spotted dinner.

Spotted salamanders can grow between 4½ in (11 cm) and 9½ in (24 cm) long.

When I spot an insect or a worm, I quickly snap it up in my jaws.

If I am attacked, a nasty-tasting poison oozes from my skin.

Can you spot me?

This Madagascan day gecko's brightly colored skin hides it perfectly among the green leaves of its rain-forest home.

The Madagascan day gecko is a type of lizard. It can grow to 12 in (30 cm) long.

slurp

After I've eaten, I give my face a good wipe with my tongue.

scaly

My toes grip so well that I can run upside-down along the undersides of branches.

Slither, slither

Frogs and newts need to watch out when this grass snake comes looking for food. If it catches a victim, it swallows it alive and whole!

Slow-worms are around 20 in (50 cm) long, but grass snakes can grow to two or three times that size.

I'm not poisonous, but if I wave my head and hiss, I can look really frightening.

I flick my tongue in and out to pick up smells from the air.

hisssssss

I'm called a slow-worm, but I'm really a kind of lizard with no legs.

Did you know...

... Snakes have no eyelids, so they never blink. They look like they are staring all the time.

My scales are smooth.

A bite to eat

Don't come too close!
These snapping turtles look
slow and harmless, but
they could easily bite
off one of your
fingers or toes!

Did you know...

... Tiny plants
called algae grow
on the turtle's shell.
This helps it to
hide among the
swamp plants.

My beak grows all
the time, so it is
always sharp and
ready to bite.

I'm not a good
swimmer, so I
usually walk along
under the water.

S t r e - t - c - h that neck!

When a fish swims past, I shoot out my long neck and gobble it up.

These turtles grow from just 5 in (12 cm) at age two to 14 in (35 cm) at age 15.

It's hard to see me at the bottom of the creek or swamp.

Open wide

Opening its huge jaws, this mangrove snake is ready to pounce. It poisons its prey, then swallows it whole.

I inject poison into my prey from my back teeth.

Come here, little bird.

Mangrove snakes can grow to 8 ft (2.5 m), three times longer than the red-sided garter snake.

Did you know...

... A snake can open its mouth wide enough to swallow things bigger than its own head!

I'm a red-sided garter snake. I like to live near water.

I can swim and climb trees.

Splash and grab

Once I've got a fish in my teeth, it has no chance of escape.

These caimans look like logs floating quietly in the water. Then, suddenly—splash! A caiman lunges forward and grabs its prey in its jaws.

I poke the top of my head out of the water to see and breathe.

... A caiman can't chew. If its prey is too big to gulp down whole, it rips off bite-sized pieces.

These caimans are babies just 18 in (45 cm) long, but adults grow to be longer than your bed.

I'm really tough! Under my thick scales, I have a layer of bony plates that protect my body.

Slowpoke

Tortoises are slow movers. They can't run away from enemies, so they rely on their shells to protect them.

These desert tortoises are 14 in (36 cm) long—tiny compared to their massive Galápagos tortoise cousins, who are 4 ft (1.2 m) long.

My shell is very strong. It's made of bones that are covered in big, horny scales.

I'm more than 100 years old. I might even reach my 200th birthday.

If I'm frightened, I pull my head and legs back into my shell.

Did you know...

... The rings on a tortoise's shell scales show its age. The more rings, the older the tortoise is.

plod, plod, plod

I don't have any teeth, but my jaws are very sharp.

Sunbathers

Lying on a branch, this green iguana warms itself in the sunshine. Its color helps it hide among the leaves.

The green iguana is 3 ft (1 m) long from nose to tail.

I can run very fast to escape from predators.

If someone disturbs me, I'll dive into the water below and swim away.

nibble nibble

I stick out this flap of skin when I want to look big and frightening.

Did you know...

... Iguanas have amazingly good eyesight. They can see another iguana more than 330 ft (100 m) away.

Hunting for dinner

Sliding quickly and silently across the rocky desert, a hungry king snake looks for a bird or lizard to eat.

Did you know...

... When a snake grows, its skin splits and falls off. This reveals a new, bigger skin underneath.

As I slither along, my scales grip the ground to stop me from slipping.

It's hard to find